Special Edition
Happy Birthday, Celtic Courier
800 years old today!

Celtic
Courier

3rd January AD 510

Andrew Langley

Raintree is an imprint of Capstone Global Library Limited, a company incorporated in England and Wales having its registered office at 264 Banbury Road, Oxford, OX2 7DY – Registered company number: 6695582

www.raintree.co.uk
myorders@raintree.co.uk

Edited by Helen Cox Cannons
Designed by Philippa Jenkins and Cynthia Della-Rovere
Original illustrations © Capstone Global Library Limited 2018
Picture research by Kelly Garvin
Production by Katy LaVigne
Originated by Capstone Global Library Limited
Printed and bound in India.

ISBN 978 1 4747 6230 4 (hardback)
22 21 20 19 18
10 9 8 7 6 5 4 3 2 1

ISBN 978 1 4747 6232 8 (paperback)
23 22 21 20 19
10 9 8 7 6 5 4 3 2 1

British Library Cataloguing in Publication Data
A full catalogue record for this book is available from the British Library.

Acknowledgements
We would like to thank the following for permission to reproduce photographs: Alamy: Chris Warham, 23 (top), Daniel Valla FRPS, 22 (t), Dundee Photographies, 23 (bottom), geophoto, 22 (b), WENN Ltd, 9 (b); Bridgeman Images: Bridgeman Images Headdress known as the Petrie Crown, Early Iron Age (bronze), Iron Age, (2nd century AD) / National Museum of Ireland, Dublin, Ireland / Photo © Boltin Picture Library, 5 (bottom), Bridgeman Images Historical reenactment: Man with fibula (brooch) holding his cloak closed, Friuli-Venezia Giulia, Italy, Celtic civilization, 4th century BC (photo) / De Agostini / C. Balossini, 18 (t); Capstone Press/Beehive Illustration, 6; Cartoon by Philippa Jenkins, 15; Dreamstime/Tolikoffphotography, 19 (t); Getty Images/English Heritage/Heritage Images, 5 (t); iStockphoto: duncan1890, 21 (b), standby, 8; Newscom/akg0images/Werner Forman, 26; Shutterstock: 1000 Words, cover (top right), 4 (t), a2iStokker, 17 (b), Afrumgartz, 27 (b), Alexander Prokopenko, cover (bottom right), Alis Photo, 25, Anneka, 4 (b), 9 (t), Artur Romanov, 11 (b), Barbora Bridges, 12, Boiko Olha, 16, Chantal de Bruijine, cover, David Peter Robinson, 19 (b), Dja65, 19 (m), FXQuadro, cover (top middle), 14, Gigi Peis, 27 (t), Igor Ivakhno, 13, Irina Borsuchenko, 21 (t), Jason Benz Bennee, 18 (b), Kachalkina Veronika, 17 (t), Labrador Photo Video, 28 (b), LifetimeStock, cover (bottom middle), 7, Marcin Wos, 11 (t), Mauro Carli, cover (bottom left), Michael Rosskothen, cover (m), Paul Vasarhelyi, 21 (t), Pavlo Burdyak, 10, subin-ch, 28 (t), Toni Genes, 18 (m), Ungor, 24, Zuzule, 28 (middle right); Superstock: John Holmes/JHOL0056, 20, World History Archive WHA_079_0911, 28 (middle left). Artistic elements: Shutterstock: donatas1205, Hoika Mikhail, vsilvek.

We would like to thank Dr Stephen Bowman of the University of the Highlands and Islands for his invaluable help in the preparation of this book.

INSIDE...

Some words are shown in bold, **like this**. You can find out what they mean by looking in the glossary.

HAPPY BIRTHDAY TO US!

Editor Duncan Daily writes:

Failte! (That's how we **Celts** say "Welcome".) This is a special birthday edition of the Celtic Courier. We're 800 years old this year!

So, we've been around for a long time. Our first edition appeared in 290 BC. But even then, the people of Britain and Ireland had already been here for hundreds of years. That's why we sometimes call ourselves the Ancient Britons. There are many different tribes of Britons, living in lots of kingdoms. And we speak many different languages.

To celebrate our 800th birthday, we've put together a selection of our all-time favourite stories. We've organized them by subject, and you can find the dates beside each article. We hope you enjoy this look at the past. Who knows what will happen in the next 800 years?

BIG NEWS

Is it a fort?
Is it a town?

Dorset, 270 BC

Maiden Castle Just Got Even Bigger!

Maiden Castle has been here for a long time. Now, after major new building works, it's the biggest hill fort in the country!

You can see the modern Maiden Castle from miles away. It stands high on a hill. Its vast walls rear up and help to keep enemies out. Behind the walls are deep ditches – and behind these are even more walls.

The new building work at Maiden Castle

The massive earthworks curve round in a huge circle. In the centre is a great open space. This is where the people of Maiden Castle live and work, safe from attack. Their brand-new homes are neat rows of round houses, and there are fenced areas for animals and food stores.

Crafty Celtic

Cork, c.AD 100

Who wouldn't want to be a king with a crown like this? The Petrie Crown is a work in a stunning new style – brought to Ireland by craftsmen from mainland Europe. Made of **bronze**, it is decorated with two bird faces and beautifully coloured in **enamel**. Irish metalwork will never be the same again.

HIT THE WOAD

The invasion that never was

by our Defence Correspondent Brian Blueface

Kent, August 55 BC

It was an amazing sight. And a terrifying one. The Romans came over the sea from **Gaul** in over a hundred ships full of soldiers. Their leader Julius Caesar aimed to invade our island.

But the Britons had one big advantage. Our warriors were lined up on top of the huge white cliffs – while the Romans were down on the sea. We must have looked pretty scary too. We were ready for battle and covered in woad, which made our bodies blue. We shouted and screamed in rage and shook our spears at the enemy.

The Romans didn't dare to land here. So they sailed down the coast to a safer beach. But they weren't there long. After a few days of fighting, a storm wrecked many of their ships. Julius Caesar knew his plan had failed and headed back to Gaul. We won't be seeing that lot again!

Rexit!

AD 410

Well, that's that. This is the end of Roman rule. Julius Caesar tried and failed to invade our island. Then, in AD 43, the Emperor Claudius succeeded. He ended up conquering most of southern Britain. Now, four and a half centuries later, the invaders have gone for good. Make up your minds!

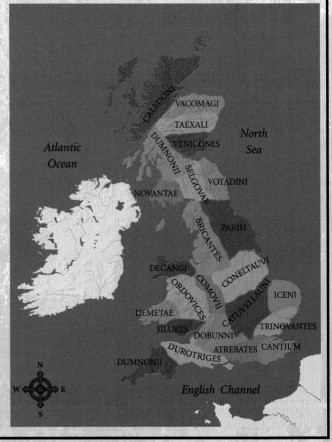

Map of Great Britain in AD 43, when the Romans invaded. It shows the tribes who were living there at the time.

WHO LET THE SAXONS IN?

Vortigern's big booboo

Kent, AD 449

Bad news for Britons. The **Saxons** are here. A huge army of them came over from Germany and settled in south-east England. Their warriors are just too powerful for us. They are taking over more and more territory. How did this happen?

Many people blame Vortigern, the ruler of southern England. Ever since the Romans left in AD 410, Britain has been a mess. **Pictish** people have swarmed down from the far north, burning and looting and killing. Nobody was able to control them.

Then, last year, Vortigern invited the Saxons to come and help. He promised them land to live on. In return, they had to drive out the pesky Picts. This was a very bad idea. Hundreds of Saxons rushed to England. They defeated the Picts, but they didn't stop there. Now Saxons are in charge of most of the south. We'll never get rid of them. Thanks to Vortigern.

RELIGIOUS NEWS

DRUIDS' DAY OF DOOM

Anglesey, AD 60

Disaster has struck Ancient Britain. The Romans have destroyed the community of **Druids** on the island of Anglesey. For hundreds of years, Druids have led us in worshipping the gods. They settled disputes and educated young people. Now they have all been wiped out.

The Romans wanted to destroy our ancient religion. They knew that Anglesey was a last stronghold – not just for Druids, but also for British **refugees**. This morning, Roman troops crossed the Menai Strait. An eyewitness at the scene, Iwan Torunaway, said:

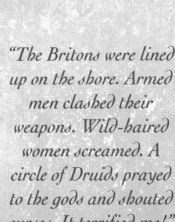

"The Britons were lined up on the shore. Armed men clashed their weapons. Wild-haired women screamed. A circle of Druids prayed to the gods and shouted curses. It terrified me!"

But not the Romans. They raised their flags and charged. Anyone who got in their way was cut down. They even set fire to the sacred woods where the Druids lived. Nearly every Briton on Anglesey was killed. Will we all have to worship the Roman gods now?

RELIGIOUS NEWS

FROM SLAVE TO SAINT

The amazing story of Patrick

Ireland, AD 461

People all over Ireland are mourning their great Christian saint, Patrick. He died this week at the amazingly old age of 74.

Patrick had a horrid start in life. Born in Britain, he was kidnapped as a boy. His captors took him to Ireland and sold him as a slave. He had to work high in the cold mountains, looking after pigs and sheep. Patrick came to think he was being punished because he refused to believe in the Christian faith. He soon became a Christian.

Later, Patrick escaped back to his Scottish home. He was free! But then he had a dream. In the dream, he heard Irish voices begging him to return and tell everyone about Christianity. He obeyed, and spent the rest of his long life in Ireland. He worked hard and inspired many people to join the faith.

HAPPY BELTANE!

1 May, 100 BC

Summer's here! It's time to get the fires lit – the fires of the **Celtic** god Bel. **Beltane**, as we call it, marks the magic moment when our farming year begins. And if some people are feeling really brave, they jump over the fire. This makes sure their crops grow well, and they'll be healthy and happy through the whole year.

BUSINESS NEWS

IRON MAN

Making the miracle metal, with Lug the Smelter

Cumbria, 500 BC

The flames crackle in the **furnace**. Lug the Smelter bends down and feeds more charcoal into the fire. His foot goes up and down, pumping the **bellows**. This whooshes air into the furnace, making the blaze roar like a dragon.

"That's hot enough,"

says Lug.

Next, he picks up lumps of rough **iron ore**, just dug out of the ground. He drops them into the clay tower above the furnace. The fierce heat from below quickly burns away the rock and other unwanted material. All that's left is the pure iron.

Lug pulls out the lump with a long pair of pincers. It's as big as a man's fist, and still glows red hot.

"There you are,"

he says proudly.

"That's what all the fuss is about."

And he's right. This is the metal that's much tougher than **bronze**. It's being made into everything from swords and spearheads to hammers and nails. It's changing our lives, all over Britain and Ireland. No wonder they call this the **Iron Age**!

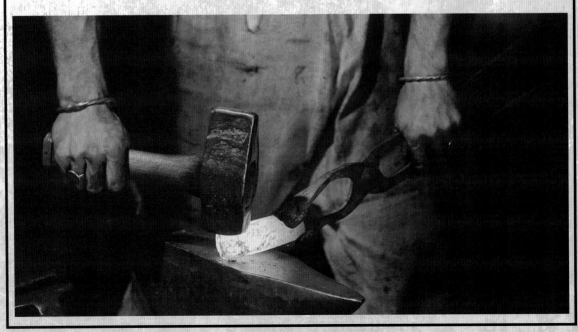

BUSINESS NEWS

LET'S TALK BUSINESS

Bridging the language barrier

Dorset, 100 BC

Once it was a quiet spit of land poking out into the English Channel. But today, Hengistbury Head on the south coast is a busy sea **port** with a big town around it.

Hundreds of traders cross the sea from **Gaul** to get here every year. They bring wine, jewellery and other luxury goods to sell. In exchange, they buy British metal, grain, leather and slaves.

So – why Hengistbury? Here's what makes it so special:

- ships can land easily on the gently sloping beach
- goods can be ferried inland along two big rivers
- the traders from Dorset and Gaul speak different kinds of **Celtic** language, but they are still able to understand each other. This makes bargaining easier!

BRITCOIN

Bredgar, Kent, 150 BC

We're in the money! For the first time, Britons have got their very own coins. They're made of gold and silver. The Gauls have been minting coins for years. They've even brought them over the Channel to spend here. But now we can buy stuff with proper home-made British cash. Nice!

FARMING NEWS

KEEP OUT THE CATTLE RAIDERS!

Dig yourself a ditch, says security expert Ivor Bigstick

Cleveland, 100 BC

Farmers, watch out! There's been a new wave of cattle stealing. Thieves have been breaking into our fields and taking our cows. It's time to protect your farm and your animals against these villains.

Here are my top anti-raider tips:

- **A big ditch**
  The best way is the simplest. Dig a ditch around your property. Make it as wide and deep as possible. Chuck all the soil into a mound on the outside. This will not only stop the thieves coming in – it will also stop your animals wandering out! (You can even put ditches in between your fields, to prevent the cattle and sheep from eating your crops.)

- **A bigger ditch**
  Dig two ditches around your property, one inside the other. Pile up earth in between the ditches and on either side, making three walls.

- **A big dog**
  Get a dog as large as a wolf. That should scare away intruders.

- **A big house**
  Keep your animals safe inside with you at night. They'll help to keep the place warm in winter.

FARMING NEWS

TOP OF THE CROPS

How farmers are growing more food

Britain, AD 50

Britain is getting crowded. We Britons have been joined by settlers from **Gaul** and Spain. Now we've got the Romans flooding in as well. How are we going to feed them all? Answer: we have to grow a lot more food! Here's how farmers round Britain are tackling the job.

Scotland

In the far north, good farmland is scarce. So farmers are creating more. They cut down huge areas of ancient woodland and use the clearings to raise cattle and sheep. They also use the land to grow more crops. They burn all the cut-down trees and stumps. The ash from the fires is good for the soil.

South-east Britain

Farmers in Kent are inventing new ways of making the land more **fertile**. They put rotting leaves and mud on their fields. Best of all, they dig chalk out of the hills (some chalk pits are very deep). The chalk is spread on the land, which makes crops grow better.

North and east Britain

Britain has a damp climate – it rains a lot! So farmers up here sow grain crops that don't mind the wet. The most popular are **barley** and **spelt wheat**. Spelt also grows better in poor soils than other kinds of wheat do.

Woof! Woof!

Southern Britain, c.AD 100

It's official – British dogs are the best! They are famous for being fast and strong – just right for chasing other animals. Even the Romans are buying our hunting dogs and taking them to all corners of their great empire.

A DAY IN THE LIFE

This week... WOMAN WARRIOR

Skye, c.AD 500

There are many stories told about the mysterious Scathach and her school. Is she a myth or is she real? They say the school's called the Fortress of Shadows. There, Scathach teaches people how to fight. And not just any people. All her pupils are learning to be heroes.

Each morning, the pupils have to leap over a huge **ravine** to reach the school. Scathach is waiting for them.

"Every day is busy," she says.

*"I teach them how to use swords, spears and sticks, and how to make magic sounds. Then there are the magic weapons, like the **gae bolg**."* What's that?

"It's a secret," she says, smiling.

But isn't this all really dangerous?

"Sometimes. But I can look after myself. One of my pupils was Cuchulainn, the great Irish hero. He wanted to show he was stronger than me. We fought for days, but at last he gave up. We stayed friends, though!"

LETTERS TO THE EDITOR

THE PAGE WHERE YOU TELL BRITAIN WHAT YOU THINK

WHAT'S WRONG WITH US?

Come on, you Romans. You've had a bash at everyone else. You've invaded Britain. You've defeated Scottish tribes and built a wall to keep them out. You've got a great big empire. So why haven't you tried to invade Ireland? I think you're scared of our mighty warriors. Pathetic, I call it.

Yours sincerely,
Enda Myshillelagh
Ballycotton, AD 85

GOOD RIDDANCE!

The Romans have gone at last. Sensible British folk (like me) have been trying to get rid of them for years. So let's all shout Hurray! Mind you, some people are moaning. They whinge on about how the Romans protected us and made us wealthy. I say "Hooey". We'll be far better off on our own.

Yours sincerely,
Boris Norris-Morris
Tunbridge, AD 410

OLD KING WHO?

Who is this Old King Cole bloke everybody's singing about? There certainly was a king once in Northern Britain named Coel the Old. His army was defeated by the Scots, and he fell in a bog and drowned. Very tragic. But as far as I know, he never had a pipe or a bowl or three fiddlers.

Yours sincerely,
Mary Hadalittlelamb
Yarm, AD 420

The invention of the coracle

CELEB NEWS

First with the latest about people who matter

CARTY AND CLAUDY
Cosy Up

Yorkshire, AD 43

The Romans just love Cartimandua. And no wonder. The queen of the northern Brigantes tribe is one of their biggest fans. Unlike most other British leaders, she quickly made a deal with the Romans. She promised not to fight against them if they would protect her.

She's become very friendly with our conquerors. In fact, some believe that the Emperor Claudius got to know the queen rather well on his recent visit to Britain. And a lot of Britons are angry. They say Cartimandua has sided with the enemy and is a traitor.

When she was interviewed recently, the queen said,

"I don't care what the Brits think. After all, Claudius thinks I'm important. He has even put an inscription about me on his famous Arch of Claudius in Rome."

CELEB NEWS

KNEEL TO NIALL

Northern Ireland, AD 445

Strongman Niall is to be the next High King of Ireland! After a sensational day here in Ulster, he was named as the successor to his father.

But the old king has five sons. Why was Niall chosen out of the five? The queen decided that there must be a contest. And it had to be a hard one. The sons were all locked inside a burning **forge**. They had to save something from the flames, then escape.

All five escaped from the forge. What had they saved? One brother had a sword, another a shield, another a pile of wood, and another trough of water. Niall staggered out carrying an enormous **anvil**, which was used for hammering out iron. He also carried a sledgehammer. He won the contest. What a man!

MAN OF MYSTERY

Somerset, c.AD 510

Who is King Arthur? Everybody's talking about this hero who led the Britons to their great victory over the **Saxons** at Mount Badon. But no one knows who he is or where he comes from. Arthur just doesn't do publicity.

FASHION HIGHLIGHTS

COMPLETELY MANTLE

Dublin, AD 400

It's bright. It's warm. It even keeps out the rain (for a while). Everyone in Dublin is wearing one: the brat is this year's must-have mantle. Made of wool, brats come in an array of colours and styles. Some are striped, some have fringes and some are speckled like a hen. Just drape it around your shoulders and pin at the front with a brooch.

TORC ABOUT PRICEY!

Norfolk, c.75 BC

Imagine you're very, very rich. How do you show off your wealth? One way is to wear a **torc** round your neck – especially one of the new torcs made in Norfolk. They're not just stunningly beautiful, they're also made of solid gold. Not many people can afford one of these.

CLOTHES TO DYE FOR

c.AD 150

Years ago, we Britons painted our bodies and faces to frighten people. Now we just colour our clothes instead – to look jolly. But we still use the same dye, which comes from the woad plant. For red, we use the Madder plant. And for yellow, there's weld. You'll find those plants growing wild.

HANDY HINTS

Nifty Nora
answers your questions

Q

I'm a potter. But the clay always goes lopsided. All my pots look uneven and silly. Nobody wants to buy them. What can I do?

A

Get yourself a wheel. By an amazing stroke of luck, potters' wheels have just been invented in south-east England. Just put your clay in the middle of the wheel, spin it around and, hey presto! Your pots will all be perfectly round and even.

Q

I've been invited to a party in South Wales. What's the right sort of present to give to the host? Obviously I can't take a box of chocolates, can I?

A

I've heard that the fashionable thing to take to parties round there is ... a pig's leg! (But make sure it's the right front leg – I don't know why.) Welsh people like to have a big feast of roasted pigs' legs at their parties.

Q

We live in a roundhouse. It gets very smoky inside, because the fire is burning most of the year. Is it a good idea to cut a hole in the roof to let the smoke out?

A

*No, it's not! In fact, it's dangerous. The hole would create a much stronger draught upwards, and the fire would get much hotter. In the end, it would set fire to the roof. Then you wouldn't have a **roundhouse** at all. Just put up with the smoke – it will find its way out through the thatch.*

TRAVEL NEWS
CORACLE MIRACLE

Travel writer Rhodri Rowlocks takes a trip in the lightest boat ever!

Ceredigion, 200 BC

The coracle is tiny. There's barely room for me to sit down. And it's a nightmare to steer. It is very light, and the slightest wind blows it about. It's round as well, so it spins in the river current.

I'm useless in a coracle. Yet Welsh people use them every day. They travel along rivers in them, and even along the sea coasts. They can steer the little boat through the tiniest of gaps and over very shallow water.

With a single oar in one hand, they can catch salmon with the other hand, using a long spear.

On the river bank, I watch a man making a new coracle. He makes a frame with small tree branches tied with rope. It looks like a big basket. Then he covers the frame with the skin from a cow. The little boat is so light he can carry it on his back.

TRAVEL NEWS
LET'S GO!

Britons flee to new homes in Europe

Cornwall, c.AD 450

Local woman Wenna Myscarpering moans:

*"I've had enough. All these Angles and **Saxons** coming over here, taking our land. I'm getting out."*

Wenna is just one of many Britons emigrating to other countries across the sea. They are worried for their safety. Saxon armies already control much of south and east Britain.

But where is she going? Wenna explains:

*"The nearest place is **Gaul**. There are plenty of Brits there already. That's why they call it Brittany. And a lot of people have gone to northern Spain. To a place called Britonia."*

CAESAR TEASER

Kent, 54 BC

It's official – Romans are scared of British chariots! Julius Caesar's soldiers have landed on our shores twice now. And both times the charioteers have attacked them. At least 2,000 horse-drawn chariots hurtled straight at the invaders. A soldier leaped down from each one, and threw a **javelin**. Every time the enemy came near, the soldiers jumped back into the chariots and raced away. The Romans were thrown into confusion. Even Caesar himself admires the skill and daring of our charioteers.

HOMES FOR SALE

Trelystan, Clwyd

Want to buy your first home? This little house is perfect for two people. Its straw roof and woven willow walls will keep you both nice and snug in winter. Once a granary (grain store), the building is raised above the ground on timber posts to keep out the damp (and the mice). The front door opens onto the single room. No windows.

Price now reduced: ~~8~~ 2 sheep

BARGAIN OF THE WEEK

Grimspound, Devon

Get away from it all! This delightful old **roundhouse** sits right in the middle of majestic Dartmoor. It is part of an exclusive estate of 24 dwellings. Everything is made of huge chunks of stone – the thick walls, the floor, the fireplace and even the beds. Now over 1,000 years old, the house is in urgent need of repair.

Price: A wagonload of firewood

HOMES FOR SALE

Lunt, Warwickshire

Live like a Roman. Snap up this beautiful gatehouse in an abandoned fort. The Romans have all gone, but they left behind lots of buildings – forts, palaces, villas and public baths. The house at Lunt Fort sits high up over a gateway in the wall. It has two floors, with stunning views in all directions. You'll need to put a roof on it, though.

Price: **100 gold coins**

Tealing, Angus

Join the **weem** team! This **Pictish** "weem", or underground house, is dug right into the earth. Inside are two curved rooms, both giving lots of space. The walls are lined with stone to stop the earth falling in, and the roof is thatched. It stays dry and warm – and it's a handy place to hide from enemies.

Price: **100 sacks of barley**

FOOD AND DRINK

SHE SELLS SEA SALT

Lincolnshire, c.400 BC   On the seashore, with Bretta the Brinemaker

Everyone needs salt. Without it, we would all be very hungry this winter. We use salt to preserve fish, meat and vegetables to keep us going through the cold months. Otherwise it would all go rotten. No salt = no food!

But where does all this salt come from? The sea, of course – because it's full of salt. But how do you get the salt out of the water? That's the job of Bretta the Brinemaker. Far away on the coast of Lincolnshire, she collects sea water in long shallow pans. The heat of the sun makes some of the water evaporate (turn to gas).

Next day, Bretta pours the water into clay pots and puts them over a fire. The water boils away, and all that's left inside the pot is a big lump of salt. When she has got enough pots, she carries the pots to market and sells them. And it's not just cooks who buy them. Medicine makers and metal workers also use a lot of salt in their work.

FOOD AND DRINK

BUBBLE BUBBLE

Wiltshire, c.200 BC

Giving a feast? Is it an important birthday? Or do you just want to show off? Then get yourself a **cauldron**. You can cook great big stews in it. Or you can heat up the drinks on a cold night. They're making them much larger and stronger these days, thanks to iron. A modern cauldron can feed a lot of people. And only wealthy people can afford to buy them. But remember – the bigger the pot, the bigger the party!

Bury Your Butter

Writes our special guest, British Food Reporter Pete Bog

Meath, AD 10

It sounds crazy. But it seems to work. Take an oak barrel and cram it full of fresh butter. Put on the lid. Then bury it in boggy, peaty ground! A month – or even a year – later, you dig it up again. By this time, it's dry and crumbly and has a brand new cheesy taste. Some say it's yummy, but others say it's disgusting. I love it. It even has my surname in it: Bog Butter!

ARTS AND ENTERTAINMENT

THE SHIELD THAT NEVER WENT TO WAR

London, c.150 BC

What's this shield for? It is a work of art. And yet it is also a weapon of war. It took a lot of time and money and skill to make it. And yet it was never finished – the **bronze** cover was never fitted onto a wooden backing.

The Battersea shield has been beautifully made. Sheets of bronze are held together with bronze **rivets** and a bronze strip all the way round it. The front has three swirly designs, made by hammering out the metal from the back. These are set with studs of red glass. Right in the centre is the **boss**.

The shield has never been used in fighting. It never will be. Instead, it will be thrown into the River Thames in a special **ritual**. This lovely object is a gift for the gods. No one will ever see it again.

ARTS AND ENTERTAINMENT
DON'T MISS THE MYTH!

Antrim, 250 BC

Here's your chance to hear the story of the greatest Irish hero of all time. All this week, celebrity bard Seamus the Famous tours Ireland and tells tales of the legendary Finn MacCool. This giant warrior performed many amazing deeds, such as:

- Catching and eating the Salmon of Knowledge, a magic fish. This gave him all the knowledge in the world
- Fighting and killing the fire-breathing monster Aillen, who had terrorised the High Kings of Ireland
- Building the Giants' Causeway by tearing rocks from the cliffs and hurling them into the sea. He wanted to cross over to Scotland without getting wet!

Lyre Lyre

Skye, c.500 BC

You don't have to sing on your own any more. A clever person here has invented something that makes music all by itself. We call it a **lyre**. It's made of wood, with thin strings fixed across. Each string makes a different note when you pluck it with your fingers. You can even play the lyre and sing at the same time! Whatever will they think of next?

FOR SALE

HOUSEHOLD

Woad face cream: two pots for the price of one!

Makes your skin silky smooth – and blue. Ideal for scaring your enemies. Made from genuine organic woad plants.

Wagon load of clay

Perfect for making pots. Buyer collects – and digs it out of the ground.

Torc is cheap

This one is, anyway. In need of repair after it was trodden on by an ox. Any offers?

The Saxon Phrase Book

Just out! Learn to talk to the new wave of German settlers. Full of useful Saxon phrases, such as "Don't hit me with that axe" and "Get off my land".

FARM AND GARDEN

Wicker Man

Giant statue made of sticks. Just like the **Druids** used to burn at festivals. Would make a perfect garden ornament.

Slingshot

Made of the finest leather, this can fling a stone a long way. Perfect for driving off wolves or bears. Can also be used in battle.

Logboat for sale

Made from a hollowed-out tree trunk. Floats well, but very heavy. Will swap for two coracles.

Puppies need good home

Genuine British hunting dogs – the best! Buy them before the Romans do.

SERVICES

Sword stuck in a big stone?

We can help you. Swords removed from stones swiftly and cleanly. Call now for a quote. King Arthur Weapon Recovery Ltd, Glastonbury

It's sheep shearing time

Time to call Fleeced Lightning, the quickest shearers in the land. With our new iron shears (just invented), we'll clip that wool off before you can say Baaa!

Chariot repairs

Broken wheel? Dented paintwork? Our skilled mechanics will solve all your chariot problems. We also do MOTs. Barry's Charries, Runcorn

JOBS

Can you pump bellows?

I'm a busy iron maker and I need help. Jobs include pumping the **bellows**, tending the **furnace** and carrying **iron ore**. Only strong willing boys and girls need apply. Call Brian at Brian's Iron, Monmouth

Can you dig it?

Yes, you can! Grab your pick and shovel and head down to Wiltshire. Hillfort Holdings are taking on diggers to build ditches and walls at the new Maiden Castle development.

TIMELINE

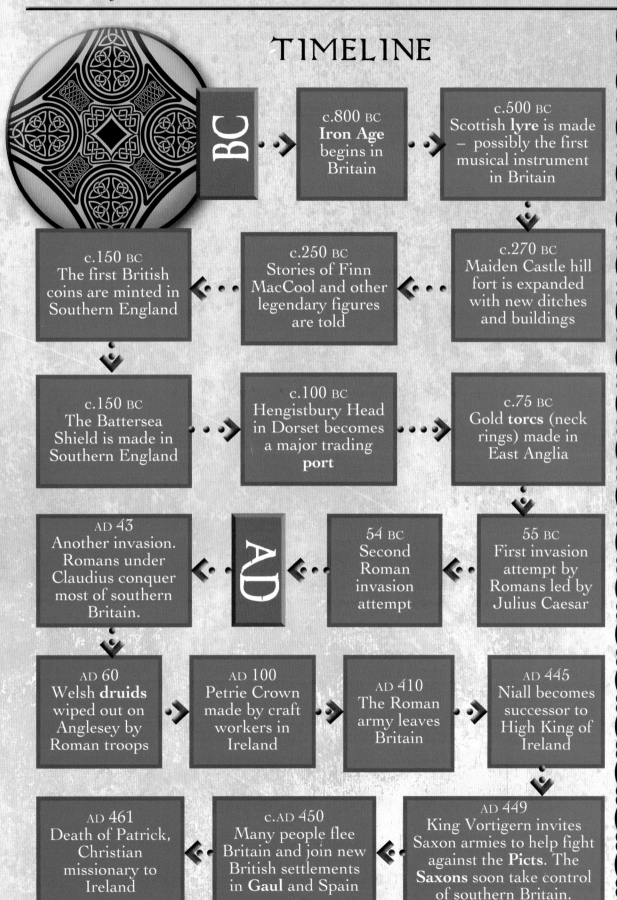

BC

c.800 BC
Iron Age begins in Britain

c.500 BC
Scottish **lyre** is made – possibly the first musical instrument in Britain

c.150 BC
The first British coins are minted in Southern England

c.250 BC
Stories of Finn MacCool and other legendary figures are told

c.270 BC
Maiden Castle hill fort is expanded with new ditches and buildings

c.150 BC
The Battersea Shield is made in Southern England

c.100 BC
Hengistbury Head in Dorset becomes a major trading **port**

c.75 BC
Gold **torcs** (neck rings) made in East Anglia

AD 43
Another invasion. Romans under Claudius conquer most of southern Britain.

AD

54 BC
Second Roman invasion attempt

55 BC
First invasion attempt by Romans led by Julius Caesar

AD 60
Welsh **druids** wiped out on Anglesey by Roman troops

AD 100
Petrie Crown made by craft workers in Ireland

AD 410
The Roman army leaves Britain

AD 445
Niall becomes successor to High King of Ireland

AD 461
Death of Patrick, Christian missionary to Ireland

c.AD 450
Many people flee Britain and join new British settlements in **Gaul** and Spain

AD 449
King Vortigern invites Saxon armies to help fight against the **Picts**. The **Saxons** soon take control of southern Britain.

GLOSSARY

anvil heavy iron block on which metals were hammered and shaped

barley grain crop, which grows well in damp or cold places

bellows pump, worked by hand or foot, that was used to push air into a furnace and make it burn more fiercely

Beltane Old British festival for May Day (the first of May)

boss bolt through the centre of a shield. The handle was fixed behind the boss so that it protected the holder's hand.

bronze metal made by mixing copper and tin

cauldron large cooking pot, often with legs underneath for standing over a fire

Celts ancient group of people from Western and central Europe. Celtic settlers probably reached the British Isles at least 3,000 years ago.

Druid priest and community leader during Iron Age Britain before the arrival of Christianity. It is believed that the Druids worshipped many nature gods.

enamel smooth glassy surface baked onto metal or pottery for decoration

forge place in which a blacksmith works, heating and shaping metal

furnace metal or earthenware box inside which a fire is built. A furnace is used to melt metals such as iron and copper.

gae bolg deadly magic spear used by the Irish warrior Cuchulainn

Gaul ancient region of Europe which covered modern-day France, Belgium, the southern Netherlands, south-western Germany and northern Italy

Iron Age period in British history, from around 800 BC to AD 43, when iron came into use

iron ore rock or mineral containing iron that is dug out of the ground. The iron ore is separated from the rest of the rock through a melting process.

javelin spear made for throwing at the enemy

lyre stringed musical instrument, similar to a harp

Picts ancient group of tribes who lived in eastern and northern Scotland during the late Iron Age

port place with a harbour where ships load and unload their cargo

ravine deep, narrow gorge or small valley

refugee person who has fled their country due to some kind of danger or disaster

ritual ceremony performed in a set way

rivet pin with a head, used to fix metal plates together by placing it through a hole then flattening the other end

roundhouse circular house, usually made of wood or stone, with a thatched roof

Saxons people from what is now Germany, who settled in Britain after the end of Roman rule

spelt wheat type of wheat which grows well in damp or cold places

torc metal ring made to wear round the neck as jewellery

weem Scottish word for an underground store room or dwelling

FIND OUT MORE

There's a lot more to discover about the Iron Age in Britain, and about the way it was shaped by the Celtic peoples of Europe. New discoveries are being made all the time. Read about them in books or online, or visit some of the sites or museums containing items from the period. Here's just a tiny selection to get you started.

BOOKS

Best-Loved Irish Legends, Eithne Massey (The O'Brien Press, 2011)

Bronze Age and Iron Age Hill Forts (Prehistoric Britain), Dawn Finch (Raintree, 2017)

Changes in Britain from the Stone Age to the Iron Age (Early British History), Claire Throp (Raintree, 2015)

Cut-Throat Celts (Horrible Histories), Terry Deary (Scholastic, 2016)

Iron Age (Britain in the Past), Moira Butterfield (Franklin Watts, 2015)

The Roman Empire and its Impact on Britain (Early British History), Claire Throp (Raintree, 2015)

WEBSITES

www.bbc.co.uk/guides/z8bkwmn
This BBC site has lots of articles, animations and videos about the Iron Age.

www.bbc.co.uk/wales/celts/
Another BBC site with even more fun and facts.

www.natgeokids.com/uk/teacher-category/stone-age-to-iron-age/
National Geographic site which gives links to loads of interesting stuff on prehistoric Britain.

PLACES TO VISIT IN GREAT BRITAIN AND IRELAND

This is a very tiny selection of places to visit, including the best museum collections. For more places, search online for Iron Age and Celtic sites in Britain and Ireland. Is there something near you?

The British Museum
Great Russell Street
London WC1B 3DG
Many treasures, including the Snettisham Torc

Butser Ancient Farm
Nexus House, Gravel Hill, Horndean, Hampshire, P08 0QE
Open-air museum, with reconstructions of prehistoric buildings

Caer y Twr hill fort
Holyhead Mountain, Anglesey, Gwynedd
Visit the island which was the last stronghold of the Druids

Hill of Tara
Castleboy, Meath, Ireland
The seat of the High Kings of Ireland

Maiden Castle
Winterborne Monkton, Dorchester, Dorset, DF2 9PT
The largest and most amazing of all the hill forts. It's always open – and free!

National Museum of Ireland
Kildare Street, Dublin 2, Ireland
Bog bodies, gold jewellery and much more

National Museums of Scotland
Chambers Street, Edinburgh, EH1 1JF
A brilliant collection of Iron Age items

INDEX